A HOLY MYSTERY

TAKING APART THE TRINITY

Topical Line Drives
Volume 34

CHRIS EYRE

Energion Publications
Gonzalez, Florida
2019

ISBNs:

Print: 978-1-63199-673-3
Kindle: 978-1-63199-674-0
iBooks: 978-1-63199-675-7
Kobo: 978-1-63199-676-4
Aer.io: 978-1-63199-677-1
Google Play: 978-1-63199-678-8

Energion Publications
PO Box 841
Gonzalez, FL 32560

https://energion.com
pubs@energion.com

THE PROBLEM WITH THE TRINITY

I'm starting to write this shortly after Trinity Sunday, one of the few days in most mainstream churches where a doctrine is associated with the day and almost always preached on, including the Anglican communion which is my current home.

All over the country, and probably the world, vicars will have been getting lay readers or fresh-faced curates to preach the sermon. Some of those vicars will have sat quietly at the back of the congregation and listened as their less experienced or less educated colleagues flounder in an attempt to talk about Trinity in a way which doesn't fall into any of the many heresies available. I like to think that for the most part they do this to offer an important learning opportunity. I suspect, however, that many do it because they fear they themselves can't make the concept accessible to the layperson without falling into one of the positions defined in the past as heretical. Or they just appreciate Schadenfreude[1]. I have myself in the past been known to take in two or three sermons on Trinity Sunday, and while my excuse is that I'm hoping to steal a new and wonderful idea for expressing the Trinity, actually I'll admit that I too enjoy a bit of Schadenfreude.

If you want an introduction to the pitfalls of the situation, a fine piece of humour from "Lutheran Satire" can be found at the footnoted address[2]. In it, two comic Irishmen ask St. Patrick to explain the Trinity to them, but claim that they are "simple people" without learning, and he should "try to keep it simple". Faced with the bald statement of three persons, but one God, they ask Patrick to use an analogy. Patrick starts with water, which can be found as liquid, solid (ice) or vapour (steam). Their immediate answer? This is modalism, condemned by Canon 1 of the Council of Constantinople of 381.

He suggests the sun, which produces light and heat, and is accused of Arianism, a heresy which states that Christ and the Holy Spirit are creations of the Father in the way that the sun produces light and heat but is not either. A three leaf clover is partialism,

---

1 A very useful German term which English has stolen, meaning "taking pleasure in the misery of others"

2 https://www.youtube.com/watch?v=KQLfgaUoQCw

which denies that there are three distinct persons and claims each is part of a greater whole. Finally, Patrick tries a man being a father, a husband and an employer, and is again accused of modalism.

Exasperated, Patrick says

> *"The trinity is a mystery which cannot be comprehended by human reason but which is understood only through faith and is best confessed in the words of the Athanasian Creed."*

and goes on to quote the relevant section of that creed. This states:-

> *That we worship one God in Trinity, and Trinity in Unity; Neither confounding the Persons; nor dividing the Essence. For there is one Person of the Father; another of the Son; and another of the Holy Ghost. But the Godhead of the Father, of the Son, and of the Holy Ghost, is all one; the Glory equal, the Majesty coeternal. Such as the Father is; such is the Son; and such is the Holy Ghost. The Father uncreated; the Son uncreated; and the Holy Ghost uncreated. The Father unlimited; the Son unlimited; and the Holy Ghost unlimited. The Father eternal; the Son eternal; and the Holy Ghost eternal. And yet they are not three eternals; but one eternal. As also there are not three uncreated; nor three infinites, but one uncreated; and one infinite. So likewise the Father is Almighty; the Son Almighty; and the Holy Ghost Almighty. And yet they are not three Almighties; but one Almighty. So the Father is God; the Son is God; and the Holy Ghost is God. And yet they are not three Gods; but one God. So likewise the Father is Lord; the Son Lord; and the Holy Ghost Lord. And yet not three Lords; but one Lord. For like as we are compelled by the Christian verity; to acknowledge every Person by himself to be God and Lord; So are we forbidden by the catholic religion; to say, There are three Gods, or three Lords. The Father is made of none; neither created, nor begotten. The Son is of the Father alone; not made, nor created; but begotten. The Holy Ghost is of the Father and of the Son; neither made, nor created, nor begotten; but proceeding. So there is one Father, not three Fathers; one Son, not three Sons; one Holy Ghost, not three Holy Ghosts. And in this Trinity none is before, or after another; none is greater, or less than another. But the whole three Persons are coeternal, and coequal. So that in all things, as aforesaid; the Unity in Trinity, and the Trinity in Unity,*

is to be worshipped. He therefore that will be saved, let him thus think of the Trinity.

Patrick is keeping it simple, you see.

This, I think, wonderfully illustrates some of the problems encountered by the lay readers and curates. It's magnificently difficult to understand.

Delving a bit further into history, St. Patrick doesn't even fall into all of the possible heresies. Historically, it turns out, most of the heresies the church has identified relate to the Trinity. Perhaps the largest number relate specifically to the relationship of Christ with God the Father (Christological heresies). Most of the rest relate more generally to the Trinity. Abelard.org has an account[3] of the major heresies which I find the most concise and general description online. The writer is not a Christian, and the account is definitely a critical one, but I think this criticism is amply justified.

Bishop John Shelby Spong, who writes from a very liberal viewpoint, says of the Trinity

> *"The Holy Trinity is a doctrine, adopted by the Christian Church in the 4th century CE, as a way of processing and understanding their experience with God. It is a product of dualistic Greek thinking which separated God from humanity; the holy from the profane; the flesh from the spirit, and the body from the soul. That was a cultural mindset and no one in that era of history knew how to step outside that frame of reference. However, that frame of reference died in that period of history we call the Enlightenment, leaving modern Christians with the impossible task of fitting a 4th century doctrine into a 21st century world view out of which it does not come and to which it cannot speak. Does that mean that the Trinitarian experience is wrong? No, I don't think it means that, but it does mean that the Trinitarian language, which we use as we to seek to relate the Trinitarian experience is simply irrelevant."*

in a blog post at "Christians Tired of Being Misrepresented"[4].

---

3 http://www.abelard.org/heresies/heresies.htm
4 https://www.facebook.com/christiansmisrepresented/
   posts/867661836604259

However, few people are as liberally minded as he is, and I think the subject needs more attention, and certainly more foundation in scripture than he gives it.

How We Got Here

My instinct on finding a puzzle is to start by finding out how it started. So, how did the church arrive in this position, of having what is generally regarded as a very important or even an absolutely fundamental doctrine, which is however extremely difficult (some would argue impossible) for even theologically trained people to understand? One, moreover, which does not yield any easy analogies or metaphors (as these all turn out to be defined as heretical)? Clearly this is important, as the vast majority of Christianity is Trinitarian. The trinity is a large element in two of the three main creeds (the Nicene and Athanasian — the Apostle's creed is only somewhat Trinitarian), and in the liturgical churches, formulae involving "Father, Son and Holy Ghost" are everywhere. Surely the idea must be useful in order to have been elevated to a doctrine? Were it merely true, but not particularly useful, it would surely be far less prominent. We should remember that no atonement theory (theory of the effect of Jesus' death) reached the heights of inclusion in a creed, whereas trinity is at least referenced in all three of those creeds.

My immediate impulse at that point (as I was brought up a Protestant) is to go to scripture, which we regard as (in some measure depending on our theological stance) revelation from God. Is the Trinity clearly outlined there?

Trinity in Scripture

Some people do say that the Trinity is clear from the wording of the New Testament, and indeed there are many passages which refer to two of the "persons of the Trinity". There is also a current of opinion that we should always look for the operation of all of Father, Son and Holy Spirit in any scripture. I consider this to be a mistake, as it requires us to insert in scripture something which may not be there on reading the actual words — we'll see if it is!

What do these scriptures actually say?

There are a very limited number of passages which refer to all three elements of the Trinity. The only one in the Gospels is Matthew 28:19. This is a baptismal formula, and merely involves baptism "in the name of" Father, Son and Holy Spirit. It does not to my eye imply three persons of one entity — one could contemplate baptism in the names of Moses, John and Jesus, for instance. While the accounts of the baptism of Jesus (Matthew 3:13-17, Mark 1:9-11, Luke 3:21-23 and possibly John 1:29-33), all involve the trio of God, Jesus and the Holy Spirit, there is no suggestion of unity between them.

1 Corinthians 6:11 is sometimes quoted in support of the doctrine of Trinity; it refers to washing, sanctification and justification in the name of Christ and the Spirit "of our God", so might at best be regarded as binitarian ("two persons"), but it really does nothing to identify "The Lord Jesus Christ" as God. 1 Corinthians 12:4-6 refers to the same Spirit, the same Lord and the same God, but on any straightforward reading seems to differentiate Spirit and Lord from God, which is obviously not what Trinitarianism requires.

Galatians 3:11-14 is also sometimes quoted; to be sure the passage mentions all three elements, but not even as all three taking action; God regards someone as justified, Jesus redeems them and we receive the promise of the Spirit. I don't see how this can be thought of as truly trinitarian. Hebrews 10:29 might be thought of as making a link of some equivalence between Son and Spirit (the first is trampled, the second insulted, possibly by the same action), but lacks any sense of identity. There is similarly no indication of any identity in 1 Peter 1:2, which speaks of the foreknowledge of the Father, the sanctifying work of the Spirit and obedience to Christ.

Finally, there is 1 John 5:7, which in the King James version reads

> *"For there are three that bear record in heaven, the Father, the Word, and the Holy Ghost: and these three are one."*

That might well seem conclusive were it not for the fact that the earliest and best manuscripts do not include the words after the first comma, which I have underlined. Bible Hub usefully has

5

several comparison passages; you can see from, for instance, the NIV, which reads only *"For there are three that testify"* and goes on to specify these as spirit, water and blood.

There is, therefore, no actual scriptural evidence of Trinity as an entity. There are, however, numerous passages referring to pairings of those or to one of the three relationships implicit in three "persons". Can we justify the doctrine on the basis of these, adding those relationships together like three sides of a triangle?

The early Church Fathers developed the idea. Can we find any extra light on things in their writings?

FATHER AND SON

To start with, at least elements of the church decided at a very early stage, before the end of the process of writing the scriptures which became canonical, that Jesus was worthy of worship, and in some cases deserving the title of "God". I do not however think that all (or, indeed, any) of the gospel writers thought of Jesus as having been "God in and of himself, co-eternal with and equal to God the Father" as the Creed puts it; certainly the authors of the synoptic gospels never attribute to Jesus any statement that he is God.

Apologists will say that one or both of the terms "Son of God" or "Son of Man" were intended to convey identity with God. However, "Son of God" was available in earlier scripture (for example Deuteronomy 32:8 or, from Jesus himself, Matthew 5:9) to mean merely favoured humans, and in particular leaders of Israel. The gospels most definitely identify Jesus as "the Messiah", and the Messiah is the paradigmatic leader of Israel, so this does not necessarily add anything to Jesus' status.

"Son of Man" (which on the face of it does not necessarily seem a high title to a modern reader) is actually more problematic; the issue is that in Daniel 7:13-14 a "Son of Man" is identified who will be given dominion over the earth, and as in Daniel 7:9 there is a reference to "thrones" in heaven. The link is made to the Son of Man sitting on the second throne — a god-like position. Although usually interpreted in Judaism merely as an elevated king of Israel, the Jewish intertestamental literature (written between the Hebrew Scriptures and the New Testament) has tendencies towards the position being rather more than that, for example a chief agent of God or, perhaps, even, an aspect of God. However, in the Aramaic of the day, "son of man" was, it seems, also a common way of just saying "man" ("bar enash" means just "man"). If the writer intended to reference Daniel, he was also using a commonplace expression which would not cause eyebrows to rise. I grant you, the evangelists do see Jesus as making ambiguous statements sometimes!

An excellent analysis of how a human figure could be thought of as divine and an argument for the thesis that the synoptic writers regarded Jesus in this light is to be found in J.R. Daniel Kirk's "A Man Attested by God" (it portrays the synoptic writers' position as adoptionist[5], which I think is correct, and as portraying Jesus as a chief agent of God rather than as God incarnate).

The writer of the fourth gospel is another matter. Merely reading John 1 will show that the author saw Jesus as at the least expressing the Logos (word), identified as being God, and being "made flesh". This chapter is commonly taken as a straightforward statement of incarnation, the Logos having become Jesus, but I think the wording capable of several other interpretations, including the kind of meaning we'd get from talking of "fleshing out an argument", hence my use of the term "expressing" there. Identity, in other words, is not at this point clear.

Even then, however, I do not personally read any of the sayings of Jesus recorded in the Fourth Gospel as him declaring outright that he was God. The one most commonly quoted is John 8:58, in which he says "before Abraham was I am", which is generally held to be referring to the self-identification of God as "I am" in Exodus 3:14 and interpreting this as Jesus saying "before Abraham was I was God" — but the syntax of the sentence does not seem to me to support this, as there is no second form of the verb "to be" (it would need to read "before Abraham was I was 'I am' "). If I assume that it *is* a reference to Ex. 3:14 and make the substitution in the wording of John 8, I read this as meaning "before Abraham was, God [was]", as the implication of a second form of "to be" there flows more naturally to my eyes than the more usually understood

---

5 Adoptionism was also declared a heresy in 798, being the concept that while born human, Jesus was adopted by God (and so became divine) either at the point of baptism, transfiguration or resurrection.

version. I therefore read it as Jesus claiming that God was a witness. The author indisputably thought Jesus to be intimately familiar with God and God's knowledge and will.

At the very least, the author is making the statement ambiguous, which would fit perfectly with the general tenor of the gospel in which Jesus regularly makes difficult-to-understand statements which are misinterpreted by Jesus' adversaries. Let's face it, had Jesus **actually** made an unambiguous statement of identity with God in the presence of, say, Pharisees, his career would have probably ended within a matter of hours, not years!

Of course, Jesus also says in this gospel (John 12:43)

> *"For I did not speak on my own, but the Father who sent me commanded me to say all that I have spoken."*

This is one of a number of statements in the gospel clearly **distinguishing** Jesus from God the Father.

So, moving from the gospels on to Acts, what did Peter have to day about Jesus' relationship to God? Acts 2:22-24 contains the first of several statements of his faith (kerygmas):

> *""Fellow Israelites, listen to this: Jesus of Nazareth was a man accredited by God to you by miracles, wonders and signs, which God did among you through him, as you yourselves know. This man was handed over to you by God's deliberate plan and foreknowledge; and you, with the help of wicked men, d put him to death by nailing him to the cross. But God raised him from the dead, freeing him from the agony of death, because it was impossible for death to keep its hold on him.""*

This, to my eyes, is a clear statement that Jesus is a man who has been glorified (as stated in Acts 3:13), rather than a second person of a triune God.

Moving on to the author of, perhaps, the majority of the New Testament, Paul's earliest statement recorded in Acts is that Jesus is the Son of God (Acts 9:20), and in his own words in what is probably his most developed theology, Romans, says (Romans 1:1-4)

> *"Paul, a servant of Christ Jesus, called to be an apostle and set apart for the gospel of God— the gospel he prom-*

ised beforehand through his prophets in the Holy Scriptures regarding his Son, who as to his earthly life a was a descendant of David, and who through the Spirit of holiness was appointed the Son of God in power by his resurrection from the dead: Jesus Christ our Lord.".

Note that this states **human** descent from David (see the genealogies in Matthew 1:1-17 and Luke 3:23-38, which are both traced through Joseph) and an elevation to the status of Son of God at his resurrection (and not earlier). This is an apparently adoptionist Christology (as was Peter's)[6].

Yes, we can find statements in other works attributed to Paul which might argue for divine status, such as statements that he has been given a name above all other names (Ephesians 1:20-21, and more clearly Philippians 2:9), implying in the minds of many theologians that this name is YHVH, and there are statements of kenosis[7] such as Philippians 2:6-7, in which are the words "he emptied himself, taking the form of a servant". (I regard Ephesians as deutero-Pauline, i.e. as not actually being the product of Paul, but Philippians is near-universally accepted as authentic and in any event bears witness to a very early formula among Christians)[8]. It seems to me that this name, however, need not be YHVH — it could merely be "El", which appears as a God-name in the early part of the Torah and is also a common element in many biblical names (e.g. Ezeki-el), so making Jesus one among a host of Biblical figures. As to kenosis, the Philippians passage reads "although he was in the form of God...", and I immediately think of Genesis 1:27, and think "But God created everyone in his image, so this is not saying as much as people might think"[9].

The deutero-Pauline epistles (those attributed to Paul but whose authorship is widely thought to be that of one of his followers) also yield Colossians 1:15-20, which introduces pre-existence

---

6 For the non-theologian, "Christology" means investigations or speculations as to the nature of Jesus.

7 ...and "Kenosis" means "self-emptying"

8 For more information on the Pauline and deutero-Pauline letters, see Herold Weiss, Meditations on the Letters of Paul, (Gonzalez, FL: Energion Publications, 2016), 2-7.

9 I'm being atypically literalist there.

reminiscent of John. Again, pre-existence does not get us as far as identity.

While still having in mind adoptionism, I note that Matthew and Luke have birth accounts which put the moment of becoming son at conception; similarly all the gospels have accounts of the baptism, and in all but John there is mention of the Holy Spirit descending and the words "You are my beloved son, with whom I am well pleased" (Matthew 3:17, echoed in Mark 1:11 and Luke 3:22); this is more or less universally considered a reference to Psalm 2:7, which reads in the KJV *"I will tell of the decree of the* LORD: *He said to me, "You are my son; today I have begotten you"*. Note the words "today I have begotten you", which I read as a clear statement of adoption at that point; it certainly doesn't fit with being begotten by the Holy Spirit, for instance. These, though not appearing in the gospels, will have been incorporated by reference, as the audience will be expected to have thought of the Psalm, which in context clearly refers to a monarch of the royal line. (For what it's worth, I also regard the accounts of the transfiguration (Matthew 17:1-9, Mark 9:2-8 and Luke 9:28-36) as relics of yet another occasion of adoption talked of in the early oral tradition.)

Now, I am not saying that adoptionism is the correct view we should take. Although I am not writing here from a purely panentheist position, as a mystic and a panentheist myself (holding all creation to exist within God and to be in a real sense the body of God, though not that God is identical with "all that is"), I consider Jesus to have been divine from birth in any event. However, I could say the same about anyone, the distinctive quality of Jesus for me being an issue of relative excellence rather than essence. Certainly any mystic with a panentheistic viewpoint would have no difficulty in saying "I and my father are one".

For what it is worth, I also find the idea of the "Cosmic Christ" as used by, for instance, Matthew Fox, useful, though I see this as an issue of the construction of concepts, a symbolic interpretation, rather than as necessarily of a description of literal reality.

I *am* however saying that it is clear from the scriptural evidence that adoptionism is a viable position to take for a Biblical theologian; several of the biblical writers clearly did take that stance and declared it in their writings during the early days of the church. This would indeed be, as the title of Daniel Kirk's book repeats, "A man attested by God". The biblical witness is not consistent in its Christology, but I think leans towards adoptionism.

I could provide texts supporting several of the other main Christological heresies, but I think I've gone far enough to demonstrate the point. That point is however also made purely by the existence of all these heresies; there is not one for which substantial foundation cannot be found in scripture.

So at this point I come to the conclusion that there was no overwhelming need for early theologians to construct a doctrine of Trinity. Could the early theologians have reached a different conclusion, one not covered by adoptionism?

OTHER POSSIBILITIES; THE ROAD NOT TRAVELLED

We can also find in previous (Hebrew) scripture that there were many options available short of some form of coequal unity between Jesus and God. As I've mentioned, the standard Jewish attitude to the "two thrones" section of Daniel was to regard the occupant of the second throne as at the most a "chief agent" of God, a position which in the non-canonical 1, 2 & 3 Enoch was occupied by Metatron. Metatron was the semi-deified form of the prophet Enoch; the position could similarly be that of an archangel. For example, Michael is also sometimes seen as a "chief agent". Jewish thinking definitely linked the occupant of the second throne with a king of the Davidic line, who would thus be God's anointed, or in other words the Messiah. It is clear that all the gospel writers thought that was an appropriate description of the importance of Jesus, but it is of course not quite a *divine* status (at least not in any exceptional way)[10].

In the family structures of the day, of course, it would have been inconceivable that a Son was not subordinate to a Father, which is likewise not coequality. Subordinationism is another heresy, being contradicted by the Athanasian creed, which was adopted widely by the mid fifth century and which I quote early in this

---

10 Again, this is a possibility explored at length in Daniel Kirk's "A Man Attested by God".

book. Equally, Judaism had no difficulty with prophets being very elevated in status, and the gospels certainly saw Jesus as a prophet. Elijah, for example, is depicted as having been bodily assumed into heaven in 2 Kings 2:11 and as being sent back by God to aid Israel in Malachi 3:23. Some Jewish thinking about the Messianic promise includes a returned Elijah as one of a set of Messianic figures; others include the Maschiach ben David and the Maschiach ben Yosef, a kingly and a priestly messiah.

FROM TWO TO THREE (OR "WHERE DOES THE SPIRIT COME INTO THE PICTURE?")

Moving on from the relationship of Father and Son, the scriptural witness is far more difficult. Indeed, if they were to pick up the New Testament oblivious of the doctrine of the Trinity, I have severe doubts that the average reader these days would determine that a triune God was witnessed to, or even arrive at the concept that the Holy Spirit was coequal with God the Father. Yes, if you are going looking for some justification of trinity, there are passages which link Father and/or Son with the Spirit[11], but only two link all three, and none of them say anything remotely like "and all three are God". The wording in 1 Peter is

> *"who have been chosen according to the foreknowledge of God the Father, through the sanctifying work of the Spirit, to be obedient to Jesus Christ and sprinkled with his blood".*

That means that there are many other interpretations other than a kind of equivalence of Father with Son and with Spirit available for the link made in these passages.

It is also clear from the Fourth Gospel that the writer regards the spirit (paraclete) as to some extent *replacing* Jesus in function, and a strong argument can be made that the writer of Luke and Acts saw them as a two-volume movement of the Spirit by the agency of Jesus from Galilee to Jerusalem in the gospel and from Jerusalem to Rome via the agency of Peter and then Paul in Acts. This, however,

---

11 Matthew 28:19 referred to above, 1 Corinthians 6:11 & 12:4-11, Galatians 3:11-14, Hebrews 10:29 and 1 Peter 1:2 are the principal examples.

did not necessitate consideration of the Spirit as a coequal third person of God — a more natural interpretation would have been an emanation, emissary or aspect of God or, indeed, as a continuing form of Jesus as in "I will send my spirit".

So, there is remarkably little directly supporting the concept of the Trinity in the canonical scriptures. My next obvious step is to look at what the early Church Fathers, the original theologians of Christianity, had to say about Trinity.

FROM SCRIPTURE TO DOCTRINE

We find that the doctrine of the Trinity in fact took some considerable time to develop. Early church writers did link the three terms Father, Son, and Holy Spirit in various passages (for example Ignatius, writing around 110 CE), but it was not until the end of the second century that Theophilus of Antioch used the term "trinity", and he was then referring specifically to God, His Word (Logos) and His Wisdom (Sophia). Tertullian, writing around 200 years after the crucifixion, was the first record we have of a trinity comprising Father, Son and Holy Spirit, using the terminology of three persons, one substance. Even Tertullian, however, was not discussing a very detailed relationship of the three.

There followed a lot of debate, and the identification of many interpretations of the basic concept introduced by Tertullian that all of the Father, the Son and the Spirit were in some way God, until the Nicene creed, proposed at the Council of Nicea in 325 and amended at the Council of Constantinople in 381, settled the major aspects of the doctrine. In the West, it was significantly later refined by the Athanasian creed, which is what the beleaguered Patrick in the piece of satire from the start of this piece ends up quoting. The preamble in the Catholic catechism stating that it is a "mystery which cannot be comprehended by human reason but is understood only through faith" is perhaps sufficient to indicate how problematic it is as a statement.

The basics of the formula come from the Greek of the Nicene Creed; there is one substance, essence or being ("*ousian*") but three persons ("*hypostases*"). There is an immediate problem, in that it is unclear to what extent there is a true distinction between *ousian*

13

and *hypostasis*, which in its root means "standing below" or "underpinning" and thence was also used in Greek for "substance" and "essence"; the distinction becomes extremely subtle. Indeed, in discussions of trinity, the term *"prosopon"* was frequently used for the "persons" of the trinity, being a term derived from masks used in the theatre. The implication of this metaphor is thus appearance and then self-manifestation. *Prosopon* usually translates into Latin as *"persona"*[12] from which we get our term "person".

The most obvious route to an easier understanding of the concept would, of course, be to follow up this "masks" concept and see the persons of the Trinity as being (for instance) the way in which a man can be at the same time son, father and husband, or the way in which water can be encountered as liquid, solid or vapour. Unfortunately, as is seen in the Lutheran Satire cartoon, this was seen as equivalent to the route adopted by Sabellius in the third century, which was fairly promptly anathematised as the heresy of Modalism. As you can see, modalism is by far the easiest of the heresies to fall into when searching for a humanly understandable way of illustrating trinity. As an aside, water might, possibly, still be an option, but only when at the triple point, which is the combination of temperature and pressure at which it can be simultaneously solid, liquid and gas. That, however, seriously undermines its utility as an analogy.

This is a particular shame, as scripture tends to show the primary expression of God in the Old Testament as being God the Father, in the Gospels as being God the Son, and in Acts and the Epistles as being God the Holy Spirit, a temporal sequence of expressions which also makes considerable sense (and is very much in accord with the ideas of John and Luke). This was, however, part of the explicit argument of Sabellius himself. It is also ironic that it seems that Sabellius was keen on using the terms *homoousian* (of the same substance) and *prosopon* (aspects or appearances), both of which later became entirely respectable parts of Trinitarian discussion.

---

12 "Persona" is also used to indicate an assumed identity, for example in literary criticism. Neither the original theatrical use nor the modern literary one would have found favour with the architects of the concept of Trinity!

Before moving on, let me just mention that there is a further wrinkle in the mental convolutions which are Trinitarian doctrine, namely that there was also a need to explain how the Son could be simultaneously God and man, which was answered by the claim that there was one person (*hypostasis*) but two natures (*physis* — a term uncannily similar in its usual meaning to *ousian*, and often translated "essence") and two wills (*thelema*). So you have one essence (substance) divided into three persons of whom one has two essences (natures) and two wills. There are some Christian churches which hold to a single nature (monophysite) and/or a single will (monothelite), but the broad current of orthodoxy both in the West and the East is dyophysite and dyothelite (two natured and two willed), so that is probably what the reader is supposed to be.

WHY STOP THERE?

So, why three and three only? As we've already seen, Theophilus of Antioch had a trinity consisting of Father, Word (Logos) and Wisdom (Sophia). This should at least make Wisdom a potential fourth candidate. As we'll see later on, there are others.

Wisdom, (Chokmah in Hebrew), is personified in Proverbs, and in Proverbs 3:19 is the statement "The Lord by Wisdom founded the earth" and then in Proverbs 8 22:31, Wisdom is made to speak of her part in the creation at length.

If this appears somewhat similar to John 1:1-14, this is unsurprising, as Philo of Alexandria, writing around the time of the crucifixion as a Jewish philosophical theologian, was conflating Logos with Sophia[13]. I think a cursory look at Philo's set of meanings of or functions of Logos will demonstrate that the author of John 1 must have had in mind Philo's thinking. Those meanings are: Utterance of God, God's mind, God's transcendent power, first-born of God, universal bond holding together the universe, immanent reason, immanent mediator of the physical universe, the angel of the Lord, revealer of God, multi-named archetype, manna i.e. divine bread, intermediary power and finally God himself.

Incidentally, as Philo was a monotheistic Jew and wished to avoid the "two powers in heaven" problem, for him the Logos was

13 http://www.iep.utm.edu/philo/#H11

only God himself in some sense, not an absolute identity. One could therefore conclude that this should also be true for interpretation of the Fourth Gospel.

This philosophical development probably accounts for the absence of any later inclusion of Sophia, though I am perhaps surprised that no explicit attempt was made by Christian theologians to equate Sophia with the Spirit. It's probably worth mentioning that the general tenor of Jewish thought repudiated Philo's conflation of Sophia and Logos, but the New Testament writers and Church Fathers seem to have followed Philo's thinking.

Spirit, incidentally, (ruach Elohim, ruach ha-kodesh in Hebrew; pneuma Theou, pneuma Christou or pneuma hagion in Greek) means equally spirit and breath in either language, and sometimes means life or essence, taking us back to one of the persons of the Trinity who share a single essence potentially actually *being* essence. The root of our own word is closely linked to that of "breath", as in "respire", so the link persists to the present era.

In addition, as I've pointed out earlier, at the very least archangels, and possibly all angels, are seen in Judaism as agents of or even aspects of God (for which "*prosopon*" might be a valid term); *micha-el* in Hebrew means "who is like God", *gavri-el* (Gabriel) means "God is my strength", *rafa-el* means "God heals". Metatron, the angelified Enoch, seen as the executive principle of God, means something like "defender" and does not include the suffix -el, which is the element meaning "God" in these names and those of most other angels. Of course, several of these angels have been incorporated into Catholic and Orthodox thinking as "saints"; clearly subordinate to God, but nonetheless partaking of some divine power.

Catholicism and the Orthodox churches may, however, arguably elevate human saints to a semi-divine status, leading to regular jibes from some Protestants that they are complete polytheists. To be fair, there seems little difference in practice (as opposed to theory) between Catholic treatment of saints and Hindu treatment of the host of Hindu Gods, which in philosophical Hinduism are seen as aspects of Brahma or Vishnu, the "One God" of Hinduism.

Catholicism in particular tends to involve particular reverence for the person of Mary the mother of God (*theotokos*), who is elevated to a position possibly above even archangels; while in theory she is subordinate to the Trinity, in practice it is hard not to see a "trinity of four" having developed. I would mention that I have some sympathy for this, as the trinity in its Protestant understanding has no female figure. Although God is sometimes described in female terms in the Hebrew Scriptures (for example, as being like a mother — and the term "*El Shaddai*", usually translated "God Almighty" could more easily be translated "breasted one"), this does not seem to have carried forward into the largely horribly patriarchal past of the church — and the present of some parts of it. Nor does the church make much of the fact that in the original language, "Spirit" is a female noun, and if it is regarded as equivalent with Sophia (wisdom), Sophia is clearly described in Proverbs as "lady wisdom"[14].

Last but not least of the possible candidates for inclusion is the figure of the ha-satan (accuser) who is clearly described in the book of Job as a major agent of God, if not a principal agent. The Jewish intertestamental literature then develops the concept, and equates ha-satan (promoted to Satan) with the Lucifer of Isaiah 14:12-14 *"How art thou fallen from heaven, O Lucifer, son of the morning!...",* reading into this a ***fallen*** angel; the power of Satan then became that of an adversary to God rather than just (as in Job) an accuser and tester of humanity, which was ascribing to him effectively Godly power without the element of subordination appropriate for both ha-satan and the angels generally.

At this point, some readers are going to be screaming at me that we are not a dualist religion, and that Satan is eventually going to be vanquished and consigned variously to everlasting torment or oblivion, and is in no way an agent of God, still less an element *of* God. The trouble is that operationally (i.e. in the way we act, rather than in the way we ostensibly think), a lot of Christianity devotes considerable time and attention to Satan, and attributes to him as many events as it attributes to God, sometimes more. Many argue that this shows better what we actually believe than what we

14 The word "Sophia" is best known for its inclusion in "Hagia Sophia", the famous church in Instanbul, meaning "Holy Spirit".

consciously think does. I have seen interesting surveys indicating that rather more people believe in Satan than in God! If we *treat* Satan as a second God and are not bi-theists or polytheists, the only avenue left seems to me to be to incorporate him.

Indeed, in Hinduism, Vishnu has his Shiva (and most polytheistic religions have at least one personalised force of evil), though in philosophical Hinduism Shiva too is regarded as an aspect of Brahman, and is more accurately described as a force of destruction rather than of evil. Taoism has its yin and yang, the positive and negative inextricably linked and each containing a little of the other, and indeed in Job 1:21, the eponymous hero says *"the Lord giveth, the Lord taketh away, blessed be the name of the Lord"* — and, we note, the taking away in Job has been done by ha-satan. Indeed, one translation of Isaiah 45:7 has God saying *"I make peace, and create evil"*.

Why do we not therefore have a "trinity" of four (or, for Catholics, five), or indeed many more if the angels were to be included? [15] After all, Judaism did not start out monotheistic; a clue can be found in the first of the ten commandments (Exodus 20:3 is one version of this); *"you shall have no other gods before me"* clearly implies that there are other gods, and YHVH has primacy. Why have we determined that the persons of the Trinity have to be coequal, rather than two being subordinate to God the Father? This is, I may point out, the heresy of subordinationism, and a major element of the Arian heresy, which came fairly close at one point to becoming orthodoxy (just prior to the Council of Nicaea, 325).

I cannot for the life of me justify rationally the theological manoeuvrings of the second-to-sixth centuries, (though I may have gleaned some insight into the philosophical reasons for this in the course of a lot of reading), so it is to be hoped that an answer will be found in the practical application of the concept.

This is unlikely to be easy. As we found at the beginning of this investigation, even well-trained clergy have difficulty in expressing the Trinity in an easily understandable form, and lay people, I find, do not tend to think in truly Trinitarian terms at all. Many evangelical churches can be found singing "Jesus is the Lord God

---

15 I can't help thinking here of my reaction when first reading Dumas' "The Three Musketeers" and finding that there were four of them.

Almighty" in the words of a recent worship song, thus collapsing the Trinity into the person of Jesus, as well as tending to ignore any human aspect of him. Some charismatic churches sound for all the world as if the only expression of God they relate to is the Holy Spirit, and in many mainline churches you might be forgiven for thinking that the Son and the Spirit are secondary add-ons to God the Father. At the most, people may concentrate for a while on just one person of the Trinity, while ignoring the others, thus arguing they adopt a modalism based on timing and need.

Are you among them?

I certainly am, to at least some extent. I am really only a believer in God courtesy of an initial peak mystical experience, since repeated a fair number of times at various levels of intensity, and that experience yields a concept of God as absolutely unitive, as well as absolutely immanent, though not in a way exclusive of transcendence. What is more, it does it with a huge element of emotionally supported self-verification. It is just not possible for me, in my deepest feelings, to consider God as dual, tripartite or multiple. Anything else must, for me, be a manner of looking at things which is nonetheless not the ultimate truth of the matter.

SOME PHILOSOPHICAL DIFFICULTIES

I also have difficulty with the language in which the doctrine of Trinity is couched, and I'm sure many if not most people in the pews have the same problem. I don't see a really substantive distinction between *hypostasis* and *ousian* both of which words are translatable as "essence". For a start, and indeed before the Church Fathers started using them technically, the two terms were more or less interchangeable. I don't see the "spirit-body" dualism which underlies a lot of this thinking either. This could found the concept that there is one spirit and three bodies, although this is problematic in the case of both the Father and the Spirit, neither of whom are conventionally supposed to be corporeal.

My own rather provisional philosophical stance is that there is "stuff" in the matter-energy continuum, and there is "pattern". The stuff in the matter-energy continuum seems, at the most fundamental level, to be something rather like waves, courtesy of

19

quantum mechanics, but this is an inadequate picture; it is also somewhat like particles, and there is a recent experiment showing that only when measured can it be said that something has behaved like a wave or like a particle (the obvious conclusion being that whatever it actually is isn't either). It is also, perhaps, a "probability density" — which is a concept which the non-physicist is likely to find totally inaccessible and, indeed, does not seem to me like anything I can really describe as "stuff" either. However, despite the fact that I do not feel we can describe it completely adequately, I think this "stuff" actually exists (and I use "stuff" because any other term I can think of comes with too much philosophical and scientific baggage). For the technically minded, this fundamental nature of things would be "ontology". My philosophy, as you may detect, is influenced by my background as a former student of theoretical physics; you are quite likely to have your own, which may well be different from mine but is still fairly unlikely to be identical to the ancient Greek stances.

Pattern is a different matter. Pattern may be static or dynamic, although Process philosophers or theologians would argue there is no such thing as static, and perhaps the theoretical physicists would agree. Pattern inevitably involves an observer; a pattern appears to me (or to you), having no actual existence as such. Indeed, what pattern exists is frequently a function of where we observe from as well as how we process the information. The wave/particle problem of quantum mechanics, to my mind, just illustrates this. This might be merely a statistical issue, (probability density again) but most scientists think not. In a layperson's terms you might like to consider those optical ilusions in which a sketch is both a rabbit and a human. In reality, it is neither, just a set of lines on a page to which we insist on giving meaning and in which we are determined to see a pattern.

Following from this, there are no patterns where there is nothing to take on a pattern. This is the case even when we *think* of a pattern; the pattern in what I tend to call "concept-space" is being created by connections of neurons in our brains, which are "stuff", and is itself just a pattern, and one which perhaps has less reality than that which we see in the outside world. This, incidentally, is why I dismiss the concept of spirit as separable from body in mind-body dualism.

The pattern is not "real", it is first and foremost an appearance, depending massively on the point of view (or method of investigation) used to perceive it. In this I distinguish it from the Platonic concept of an "Ideal". Patterns which purport to be general are in fact models, and a model has validity only so far as it is useful, or in other words so far as the model produces the same results as are observed. For the technically minded, this all makes me (probably) a constructive empiricist.

Within this philosophical framework, it is not possible for me to make an useful distinction between *hypostasis* and *ousian*, or indeed *prosopon*, *physis* or two other terms, *morphe* (the word translated "form" in "form of a servant" in Philippians 2:6-7) and *eikona* (image, from the Greek of the Septuagint version of "the image of God" in Genesis 1:26). For me, these are at best distinctions without a difference.

I can, however, consider the use of (say) the body-spirit duality concept as having some traction, though not being the best (i.e. the most useful), as a way of ***viewing*** the situation. Similarly, I can see merit in "We hold these truths to be self-evident, that all men are created equal, that they are endowed by their Creator with certain unalienable Rights, that among these are Life, Liberty and the pursuit of Happiness" even though it seems self-evident to me that men are born vastly different (i.e. not at all equal) and subject to a large number of restrictions on their liberty, not least dependence on others in order to exist, assuredly so in their infancy, and arguably so throughout life for most of us. Although this equality ***is not*** the case, there are abundant reasons for acting ***as if it were*** the case. The trouble with the mass of "person" or "essence" type terms in Trinitarian theology is that I can't readily even see minor use in thinking this way unless it's in thinking modalistically.

I also consider that we process our experience according to the language we have available, and that includes not just vocabulary but also concepts (more complicated patterns which need several words to describe them). I don't go so far as to espouse the strong form of the Sapir-Whorf hypothesis, which suggests that the available language we have *entirely* determines our thought, but certainly have experience of the fact that at the very least our communication and expression of our experience is governed by the terminology we have available (a weak form of the hypothesis). I think differently in English and in French, for instance, and have written extensively about my problems in finding language in which to express my first peak mystical experience (as I hadn't incorporated any religiously-derived language into my instinctive thinking at the time). This, it seems to me, is at the root of the irritating habit of philosophers of making up masses of new terminology when they find their existing language and concept structures don't quite fit. Most of the time, it seems to me that this results from a paucity of vocabulary rather than an absolute need to use a new term, but most philosophers will not agree with me!.

As a result, I reject both Plato's idea that the "forms" (which were probably for him what patterns are for me) which we talk of are perfections of which material reality is a shadow[16], and Aristotle's idea that when we observe patterns we are observing the actual reality[17]. For me, the patterns we see and talk of are invented abstractions dependent in large part on our perception, and most probably simplifications, so inevitably somewhat inaccurate. Both philosophical traditions tend to result in us considering that the real world is an imperfect representation of the models in our thoughts, whereas the models are, to me, imperfect representations of the real world. The best we can achieve is that the patterns we talk of, our models of what actually is, can be refined progressively to produce better and better (i.e. more and more useful) descriptions of and predictions about the real world, but we can never say that they are what is actually happening.

The trouble is, the writers of the New Testament had only Platonic, Aristotelean and (perhaps) Jewish philosophical concepts to work with. The Church Fathers added Neoplatonism. Now, Neoplatonism ought on the surface to be attractive to me, given that its most celebrated early exponent was Plotinus, and he clearly talks from unitive personal experience of God — and so do I. Un-

16 Plato's successors in this kind of thinking are commonly called "Idealists" in philosophy.
17 Aristotle's successors are commonly called "Realists".

fortunately neoplatonism then starts from the assumption that this experience is direct experience of ultimate reality and that you can then deduce everything else from that starting point, irrespective of any other evidence, or any other experience. This is a trap into which it seems to me most philosophical theology has been falling ever since Paul was writing the first theology. It's a trap which I might be very prone to fall myself, given that the unitive mystical experience does deliver inner certainty about the truth of some of its aspects, such as the overwhelming unity and absolute immanence of deity. I cannot, for instance, seriously *feel* that "everything is within God and is God" is not true — though I can certainly **think and write** as if it might not be. Indeed, I think I have to on occasion, in order to be intellectually honest in considering other concepts.

This is, incidentally, a situation well known to philosophical theologians, who would, however, hold that while the actual nature of things (ontology) may not be understandable through its appearance, it is communicated by divine revelation. I comment merely that even divine revelation has to pass through some form of sensory perception and a human mind shaped by its available language and concept structures.

These philosophical stances also led to the ideas that God must be "simple" (i.e. not analysable into parts), thus making partialism and modalism problematic, and that God must be immutable, making any thought of change in time, such as adoptionism or temporal modalism, things to be avoided. To me, anything which cannot be analysed is something which cannot be known at all, while to the physicist or process philosopher/theologian, the concept of something which is entirely static is incoherent; there cannot be anything which is entirely static. Even atoms are only immobile at a theoretical Absolute Zero which cannot, in practice, be reached.

If we do not have the same philosophical stances, might we not think about revising our opinions of what is and what is not heretical and recognise that multiple interpretations might have some validity?

So, where does that leave us with the classic formulation of Trinity? Well, I am perhaps encouraged by the preamble from the Catholic catechism (to which Patrick refers in the Lutheran cartoon)

> *"But his inmost Being as Holy Trinity is a mystery that is inaccessible to reason alone".*

I think, frankly, that they should probably have stopped there, rather than ending up with documents as complex as the Athanasian Creed or the remainder of that section of the catechism.

Where I can support the idea that, say, adoptionism or subordinationism is a heresy is when it is stated as being ***the only and the whole truth*** — and some time ago, I wrote a blog post titled "The heresy of all doctrine"[18], the basic thesis of which was that we should not state with absolute authority things about God which, given the nature of human thought and reasoning, are at best partial truths and at worst dangerously incorrect. The best and worst can be the same statement! I would similarly say that to describe, say, an electron as a particle was partially true but potentially dangerously incorrect, just as I would say that about a description of an electron as a wave.

So, my suggestion is that we regard things as heresies only when they are claimed to be the one and only truth of the matter.

We can then look at operational definitions of Trinity, by which I mean "how people actually act as if God is" as partial (and therefore in at least some sense "wrong") but nevertheless constructive descriptions. Classic Trinitarian thought tends to hold that a doctrine of Trinity should tell us about how God is (ontology) rather than about how he appears (phenomenology), but in my philosophical framework (and quite a lot of other modern philosophical frameworks) all that we can in fact talk about is how God appears, as anything else is strictly transcendental and thus prima facie unknowable and unprovable.

It is worth pointing out here that quite a number of theologians since the late 19th century have developed the concept of the

---

18 http://eyrelines.energion.net/?p=208

"Economic Trinity"[19]. (Arguably, some earlier theologians might qualify, but the term appears to be recent). This distinguishes on the one hand between a doctrine of how God is in God's self (onto-logical or transcendental trinity), under which the various heresies and caveats I dealt with earlier are valid, and on the other hand how God is in God's relation to the world (called immanent or eco-nomic trinity); in this second sense, the considerations against any appearance of modalism are thought not to apply; the appearance is not the reality. A not very philosophically-minded reader (and I include myself in that category) might be tempted to think that this is actually a work-round, the ideas of modalism being just so strong and so well scripturally supported that they have to be adopted in some way. So might a more philosophically minded reader if they were one of several forms of realist (in which case the appearance would *be* the reality); there are other shades of philosophical stance which would have similar problems[20].

UNITARIANISM?

Now, above we have seen how various groups of Christians act as if there are in fact four, five or even very numerous ways in which God can be seen as acting (granted that some are generally seen as subordinate — notably Satan). Some groups of Christians on the other hand, for instance Unitarians, Jehovah's Witnesses, Mormons and Oneness Pentecostals, have in fact, abandoned the concept of trinity as outlined in the "orthodox" conception. I have no problem with these on the basis of their conceptions of the multiplicity or non-multiplicity of God, although I do have reservations about the good sense in elevating a concept of evil (ha-satan) to divine status as I think much of Western Christianity does operationally (i.e. in the way they act), even if they would deny the concept. I don't see that this is a route which people in denominations which

---

19 Catherine Mowry LaCugna in "God For Us" has perhaps the best extended treatment of this concept which I am aware of.
20 An idealist, however, would be able to distinguish the "form" as entirely distinct from the appearance and would be more comfortable with this thinking.

have accepted a trinity for many hundreds (or thousands) of years can now adopt, however. Could you?

SOMETHING TO BE AVOIDED

It is unfortunately very easy to take the Athanasian creed's definition of the Trinity, not understand it (consistent with the statement in Lutheran Satire's account "*The trinity is a mystery which cannot be comprehended by human reason but which is understood only through faith and is best confessed in the words of the Athanasian Creed*") but still cling to it as a form of wording which it is just necessary to learn and, if not "believe" in the normal sense, accept as true and, in some way, fundamental. To me, this is not an adequate position; it is far too reminiscent of the well known feature of sects that they demand adherence to something which, to the outside world, appears crazy, and which then serves as a distinguishing mark. It seems to me that if we can reduce it to words at all, those words must make rational sense, otherwise they are little more than a mantra, a set of sounds without real meaning.

SOME POSSIBILITIES

I am hard pressed to explain it, but there does seem to be an historical tendency to group deities in threes in many religions. Perhaps, therefore, there is something about the number three which is particularly attractive to some aspect of human psychology.

The most clear example (and the closest to a Trinitarian equivalent) is the rather common view of a triple Goddess, often as maiden, mother and crone, which is seen prominently in Wicca but also in a large number of pagan religions, including in the case of the Greeks some ideas of Artemis. These are explicitly modalistic.

One can also think of Isis, Osiris and either Set or Horus in Egyptian religion; the Greeks had a triad of Zeus, Athena and Apollo (and many other triads); the Romans had Jupiter, Juno and Minerva (among others); the Norse had Thor, Freyr and Odin and others; the early Hindus Brahma, Vishnu and Shiva inter alia. There are multiple other examples. These others must (with the exception of philosophical Hinduism), however, be regarded as tritheistic, i.e.

involving three separate gods, rather than just modalistic, and are therefore even harder to inject into a notional monotheism.

It is not just deities which are thought of in threes either. There are three Fates, three Graces and three Furies in Greek mythology (and a three-headed dog), and three Norns in Norse mythology. Charms in folk magic are often spoken three times, which may have given rise to the saying "anything I say three times is true", though I think that is independent. There is just something about the number which resonates with humanity in a special way, and I really can't give an explanation.

Going along with the exponents of the Economic Trinity, therefore, what I think does need to be re-explored is modalism. I would not myself, however, necessarily confine this to dealing merely with appearance. As I've said, those Christians who actually do think seriously about God as triune have a strong tendency to think of modalistic analogies in any case — a man as father/son/employer, for instance, or water as water/ice/steam. This makes the majority of Trinitarian Christians into operational modalists, and I think a doctrine observed more in the breach than in the observance is perhaps due for reconsideration, even if trinity itself is too solidly part of tradition to be abandoned.

In addition, the authors of the Trinitarian theory insisted on the persons of the Trinity being coequal. This has led to the statement that in any case where one of them is at work, so are the other two. That in turn means that unless you break the mould of avoiding modalism at all costs, you are left with no real functional distinction between Father, Son and Spirit; it is truly a distinction without a difference. It also does severe violence to one's scriptural interpretation when you always try to find all three persons of the Trinity active in situations where at most one or two are mentioned.

That said, perhaps some could join me in saying, if not that a doctrine of that-which-is-God (i.e. an ontological statement about God) is impossible to state with any confidence, then *defining* that-which-is-God is beyond our pay grade. To understand various ways in which God relates to us is, however, entirely practical, and to regard those as modes is, under the concept of Economic Trinity, now sort of acceptable.

TEMPORAL MODALISM

The temporal form of modalism, i.e. that God manifests first as the Father in the Hebrew Scriptures, then as the Son during the ministry of Jesus, then as the Spirit from Pentecost onwards, is amply supported by scripture (granted that the Spirit puts in a few earlier appearances, for instance at creation in Genesis 1 and at the baptism of Jesus in the Synoptic gospels). It is almost certainly the underlying concept behind the Luke/Acts two-part story.

Indeed, I think that if we cling desperately to the classic "one substance, three coequal persons" way of thinking, we will misread the temporal modalism of Luke's basic thesis, and also the adoptionism of his baptism story in Luke 3:21-22 and the subordinationism of his last words as Luke records them in 23:46[21]. Luke is clearly not afflicted by the need to have only one picture of God's relationship with Jesus and with the Spirit — indeed, there is a potential second moment of adoption in Luke 1:35. There are a host of other examples where we are likely to misread texts (such as those I looked at earlier when considering the scriptural basis of adoptionism) if we hold to the classic formula too tightly.

OBJECTIVE, SUBJECTIVE AND RELATIONAL

There is, for instance, a potential attraction in regarding the three persons as expressing the objective (God the Father), the subjective (God the Holy Spirit) and relational (God the Son)., otherwise "God out there", "God in me" and "God in others", the last of those with a nod to Matthew 25:44-46

> *"Lord, when did we see you hungry or thirsty or a stranger or needing clothes or sick or in prison, and did not help you?"*,

which, as a panentheist, I tend to interpret literally.

---

21 Academic Trinitarians will generally say that evidences in the gospels of subordinationism only attest that Jesus-as-man was subject to God, while maintaining that Jesus-as-Christ is coequal, a formula I find very difficult to swallow, as it gives Jesus, in effect, a split personality, leading to all sorts of problems related to how the two interacted.

This combines quite nicely with the temporal modalism which I outlined earlier; the objective God exists throughout scripture, the relational God is seen in the life and ministry of Jesus, and the subjective God is seen in the working of the Holy Spirit in individual believers and in the church generally.

INVITED INTO RELATIONSHIP

Another, currently popular, way of thinking of the trinity is as demanding relationality as a fundamental characteristic of God. Karl Barth wrote:- "

> As God is in Himself Father from all eternity, He begets Himself as the Son from all eternity. As He is the Son from all eternity, He is begotten of Himself as the Father from all eternity. In this eternal begetting of Himself and being begotten of Himself, He posits Himself a third time as the Holy Spirit, that is, as the love which unites Him in Himself".[22]

There is thus a pre-existing relationship implicit within that-which-is-God, (the technical term for which is "hypostatic union") into which the believer is invited, a way of joining in which is fundamentally communal, and which therefore particularly supports the concept of the community of believers (i.e. the Church).

It does, however, suffer from the possible objection that in order to have any validity, it has to posit not merely something which could be seen as modalism (in the sense of Economic Trinity) but actual tritheism, i.e. the existence of three Gods (as it is difficult to envision a set of relationships unless there are actually three individuals). There is also a potential difficulty in elevating the love uniting two people into another person; I might however venture to suggest that two people in relationship become, collectively, a third person (and yes, I have in mind the model of a marriage; Mark 10:7-9 says

> *"For this reason a man will leave his father and mother and be united to his wife, and the two will become one flesh.'*
> *So they are no longer two, but one flesh. Therefore what God has joined together, let no one separate.)*

---

22 Karl Barth: *Church Dogmatics vol. 1 p. 483.*

In this sense, trinity forms a template for marriage, which I find particularly satisfactory.

To distil that down, in other words, the basic concept of a relationship *implies* the number three.

You can also achieve this from merely positing that there is X (used in a quasi-mathematical sense). In order to conceive of X, it is necessary to conceive of not-X, and it follows that there must be (X plus not X), which is a third concept. One could see in this echoes of Derrida's "différance"[23]. However, you can also repeat the process and, indeed, given X and not-X, there is a relationship between X and not-X, there are relationships between (X and not-X) and X, and between (X and not-X) and not-X. It is trivial to see how this kind of thinking can give rise to a multiplicity as large as you might wish! This way of thinking has proved attractive to a few mathematically-inclined friends, though of course it suffers from all the perils of falling into a heresy unless the concept of Economic Trinity is used, and it can definitely be seen as more going to the substance than the appearance. A similar concentration on number is, however, used by Richard Rohr[24] to argue that for a Trinitarian, binary oppositions become impossible (as there is always a third), and so violence towards the other can be restrained. I do like his conclusion, though I am sceptical as to whether this is only achievable by positing the Trinity!

I have also found philosophers attracted by the "three-ness" of the dialectical process; thesis-antithesis-synthesis. I don't myself find this very helpful, but it is certainly a way in which, in processing information (thinking "Economic Trinity") we impose three-ness on reality.

Peter Rollins[25], and many other philosophers writing in the Continental tradition, also talk of the objective, subjective and

23 An invented term playing on the fact that the word is pronounced the same as the French word for difference, which also means "defer" and suggesting in one word Derrida's concept that words are never transparent without additional explanation, that explanation being deferred until they can be further explained.
24 In a talk viewable at https://www.youtube.com/watch?v=MnTC4NNIACk&sns=fb
25 He talks about "the event" in a short video at https://www.youtube.com/watch?v=iCFU2N-c1qw

"eventual", where "eventual" refers to the transformation produced by the objective and subjective working in you. This is Trinitarian in a sense, but obviously not simply reducible to either an ontological or a modalistic trinity.

BRIDGING THE GAP

I think it is also viable to consider drawing from the idea of Jesus-as mediator to think of the Father as representing God-as-transcendent (i.e. wholly above and separate from humanity), the Spirit as representing God-as-immanent and Christ as representing the confluence of the two, the mediator between heaven and earth. I'd like to introduce a note of caution here, though. This is possibly not just a matter of identifying the ways in which God appears to us, thus allowing us to say that it is an expression of the Economic Trinity; transcendence and immanence are fundamental properties, and they are in any normal conception irreconcilably different. If we are to make use of this concept, therefore, I think we need to shrug off the charge of modalism and say that is an outmoded concept, and that we should now be allowed to be modalist, perhaps with the caveat that whatever we say cannot capture the fullness of that-which-is-God, and therefore this is somewhere between just an appeal to appearance and an ontological statement.

But then, a mediator between the transcendent and the immanent is also caught between two states, so perhaps this is a workable idea after all.

OTHER POTENTIAL THREE-NESSES

For the sake of completeness, since Freud we have had a basic psychological system which is three-fold, the division of the mind into id, ego and superego. The more recent transactional analysis in psychology talks of parent, adult and child. I regard these more as other examples of the human tendency to find threes everywhere than as useful analogies for Trinity, but there you have it.

There is also the system in linguistic analysis of the signified, the signifier and the sign (which comprises signified and signifier), but this really does not achieve anything even remotely approaching three equal appearances. Followers of Lacan will also be familiar with his three orders of existence, the imaginary, the symbolic and the real. It is conceivable that a Lacanian could link this reasonably with the concept of Trinity; sadly I am not familiar enough with Lacan to comment more!

CONCLUSION

If we are members of Trinitarian churches (and the vast majority of Christians are), the traditional formulations of the doctrine are not really fit for purpose any more. Most of us either don't know the Athanasian creed or don't really understand it, and those who do, if they have any reasonably modern philosophical stance (later than, say, around 1700) will have problems making it mesh with the rest of our thinking.

It is perfectly possible, I think, to say that God is one and yet God is three persons and to stop there; any further analysis is something which we can conclude that we cannot delve into and need not think about; it is a mystery. There really is no need to go beyond that into careful formulations which end up with us saying "it is a mystery" anyhow. This may not satisfy many of us, but if God is not a mystery, nothing is.

If, however, we decide that the traditional declarations of the various heresies can be thought of as only condemning statements which try to define God as God is in Godself (ontology), rather than God as God appears to us (phenomenology), then we can adopt the idea of the economic trinity, or merely consider that those who condemned the heresies were talking about something we are not dealing with, perhaps on the basis that it is completely beyond us to define God in any ontological way. Thence a whole range of possibilities becomes open to us, many of which open up passages of scripture which otherwise seem problematic. With the economic trinity, or with the acknowledgement that we are only talking of appearance, modalism, adoptionism and subordinationism are no longer threats to our orthodoxy.

Assuming, that is, that we want to attempt orthodoxy.

And, let's face it, people thinking about God (or gods) have been thinking in threes in very many religions other than Christianity. There's just something about three. We don't *absolutely* need to understand why...

TOPICAL LINE DRIVES
Straight to the Point in under 44 Pages

All Topical Line Drives volumes are priced at $4.99 print and 99¢ in all ebook formats.

Available
The Authorship of Hebrews: The Case for Paul   David Alan Black
What Protestants Need to Know about Roman Catholics   Robert LaRochelle
What Roman Catholics Need to Know about Protestants   Robert LaRochelle
Forgiveness: Finding Freedom from Your Past   Harvey Brown, Jr.
Process Theology: Embracing Adventure with God   Bruce Epperly
Holistic Spirituality: Life Transforming Wisdom from the Letter of James
     Bruce Epperly
To Date or Not to Date: What the Bible Says about Pre-Marital Relationships
     D. Kevin Brown
The Eucharist: Encounters with Jesus at the Table   Robert D. Cornwall
The Authority of Scripture in a Postmodern Age: Some Help from Karl Barth
     Robert D. Cornwall
Rendering unto Caesar   Chris Surber
The Caregiver's Beattitudes   Robert Martin
What is Wrong with Social Justice   Elgin Hushbeck, Jr.
I'm Right and You're Wrong   Steve Kindle
Words of Woe: Alternative Lectionary Texts   Robert D. Cornwall
Stewardship: God's Way of Recreating the World   Steve Kindle
Those Footnotes in Your New Testament   Thomas W. Hudgins
Jonah: When God Changes   Bruce G. Epperly
Ruth & Esther: Women of Agency and Adventure   Bruce G. Epperly
Constructing Your Testimony   Doris Horton Murdoch

Forthcoming
God the Creator: The Variety of Christian Views on Origins   Henry Neufeld

(The titles of planned volumes may change before release.)

Generous Quantity Discounts Available
Dealer Inquiries Welcome
Energion Publications — P.O. Box 841
Gonzalez, FL 32560
Website: http://energionpubs.com
Phone: (850) 525-3916

from
inspiration
to
understanding

reading the bible
seriously and faithfully

Edward W. H. Vick

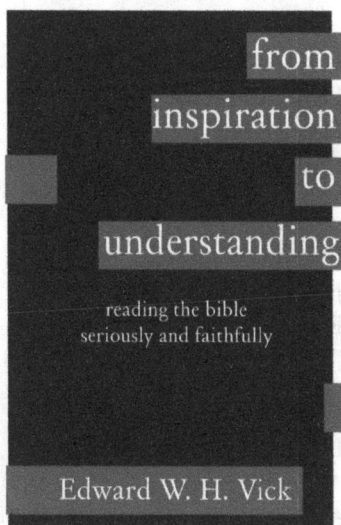

Seldom does one read so thought-
ful, so disciplined and so scholarly
an account of the need to rethink
the basis for the authority of Scripture in the Christian church.

James J. Londis, Ph.D.
Kettering College

ALSO BY STEVE KINDLE

STEVE KINDLE

I'M RIGHT
AND
YOU'RE WRONG
WHY WE DISAGREE ABOUT THE BIBLE
AND
WHAT TO DO ABOUT IT

This one hits it out of the park.

David Alan Black
Dave Black Online
http://daveblackonline.com/blog.htm

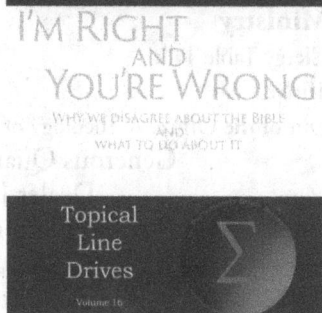

Topical
Line
Drives
Volume 16

MORE FROM ENERGION PUBLICATIONS

Personal Study
Holy Smoke! Unholy Fire	Bob McKibben	$14.99
The Jesus Paradigm	David Alan Black	$17.99
When People Speak for God	Henry Neufeld	$17.99
The Sacred Journey	Chris Surber	$11.99

Christian Living
Faith in the Public Square	Robert D. Cornwall	$16.99
Grief: Finding the Candle of Light	Jody Neufeld	$8.99
Crossing the Street	Robert LaRochelle	$16.99
Life in the Spirit	J. Hamilton Weston	$12.99

Bible Study
Learning and Living Scripture	Lentz/Neufeld	$12.99
Inspiration: Hard Questions, Honest Answers	Alden Thompson	$29.99
Colossians & Philemon	Allan R. Bevere	$12.99
Ephesians: A Participatory Study Guide	Robert D. Cornwall	$9.99

Theology
Christian Archy	David Alan Black	$9.99
The Politics of Witness	Allan R. Bevere	$9.99
Ultimate Allegiance	Robert D. Cornwall	$9.99
From Here to Eternity	Bruce Epperly	$5.99
The Journey to the Undiscovered Country	William Powell Tuck	$9.99
Eschatology: A Participatory Study Guide	Edward W. H. Vick	$9.99
The Adventist's Dilemma	Edward W. H. Vick	$14.99

Ministry
Clergy Table Talk	Kent Ira Groff	$9.99
Thrive	Ruth Fletcher	$14.99
Out of the Office: A Theology of Ministry	Bob Cornwall	$9.99

Generous Quantity Discounts Available
Dealer Inquiries Welcome
Energion Publications — P.O. Box 841
Gonzalez, FL_ 32560
Website: http://energionpubs.com
Phone: (850) 525-3916

www.ingramcontent.com/pod-product-compliance
Lightning Source LLC
Chambersburg PA
CBHW011749020426
42331CB00014B/3338